IMAGES
of America

ROUTE 66 IN
MADISON COUNTY

The diagonal path of Route 66 across Madison County is shown on this 1956 Standard Oil Company map. The approximately 40 miles, depending on the alignment, of the famous highway that cut through Madison County from northeast to southwest was the last opportunity for motorists to experience the hospitality, pleasant rural scenery, and unique combination of roadside attractions in Illinois before crossing into Missouri. (Author's collection.)

ON THE COVER: Harry Baumgartner opened the Green Gables Tourist Court between Hamel and Edwardsville in 1931 with the intent of making it one of the most popular lodgings between St. Louis and Chicago. He died eight years later from burns suffered while kindling a fire with coal oil. His wife, Floy, found him and extinguished the flames, but it was too late. A 1942 advertisement in the *Edwardsville Intelligencer* announced that Green Gables service station and tourist camp were open under new management. (Courtesy of Florence Nemnich.)

IMAGES
of America

ROUTE 66 IN MADISON COUNTY

Cheryl Eichar Jett

ARCADIA
PUBLISHING

Published by Arcadia Publishing
Charleston SC, Chicago IL, Portsmouth NH, San Francisco CA

Printed in the United States of America

Library of Congress Control Number: 2010924240

For all general information contact Arcadia Publishing at:
Telephone 843-853-2070
Fax 843-853-0044
E-mail sales@arcadiapublishing.com
For customer service and orders:
Toll-Free 1-888-313-2665

Visit us on the Internet at www.arcadiapublishing.com

For Tom and Erica

CONTENTS

ACKNOWLEDGMENTS

A huge debt of thanks is owed to Madison County Historical Society for their always-outstanding assistance and enthusiasm. Thank you also to the following institutions, without which this book could not have been completed: Cahokia Mounds State Historic Site, City of Edwardsville, Collinsville Historical Museum, Livingston Centennial Committee, and Village of Hamel. Thank you as well to the following individuals, whose contributions ranged from photographs and postcards to stories and references to proofreading, editing, and general support: LaVerne Bloemker, Debbie Caulk, Miles Dudley, Mark "Sparky" Eddleman, Michael Gassmann, Florence Gillig, Rich Henry, Nancy Hess, Bill Iseminger, Erica Jett, Bill Meyer, Sue Minner, SJ Morrison, June Nealy, Florence Nemnich, William A. Raia, Cindy Reinhardt, Steve Rezabek, Darren Snow, Joe Sonderman, Michael A. and Carol Sporrer, Michele Fischer Stark, Peter Stork, Neal Strebel, Mary Westerhold, Karen Wiesemeyer, and Brenda Whitaker. And as always, many thanks to my editor, Jeff Ruetsche, and my publisher, John Pearson, for another opportunity to share local history, and to my family for their unending love and support. To Jim Lask, thank you for the love in everything you do.

INTRODUCTION

Route 66 zigzagged across Madison County from northeast to southwest, covering terrain that included gently rolling farmland, the Mississippi River bluffs, and the fertile floodplain known as the American Bottom. As in most of Illinois, the scenery along Route 66 in Madison County was predominantly rural with villages and small cities sprinkled along the original routes. Mom-and-pop hospitality businesses, such as lodging, restaurants, and service stations, sprang up along the way, just as they did elsewhere along the famous highway; however, Madison County offered a unique variety of roadside sites. In addition to Meramec Caverns barns, neon signs, and Midwestern roadside architecture, this fourth-oldest county in Illinois claimed a Mississippi River bridge with a 22-degree bend, the largest man-made earthen mound in the Americas, and a blue neon cross. Madison County was, with the exception of short dips south into St. Clair County to cross bridges, the last chance for westward travelers on Route 66 to inhale Illinois air before crossing the Mississippi River.

The idea of well-paved roads in a thoughtfully conceived highway plan undoubtedly occurred to virtually every road traveler in the United States long before it actually happened. A national Good Roads Movement began in the late 1800s, led by cyclists advocating improved roads on which to ride their bicycles and for the good of rural populations. As the interest in the automobile grew, motorists began to lobby for some sort of national road system to link population centers and enhance the economy. On December 12, 1914, the American Association of State Highway Officials (AASHO) was founded to begin planning for a federal highway system.

Cyrus Avery, known as the "Father of Route 66," was an insurance agent and oil investor in Oklahoma who became impressed with the Good Roads Movement. He was elected chairman of the Tulsa County Commission, promoted improvement of Oklahoma roads, and became involved with various highway organizations. By the early 1920s, he was president of the Associated Highway Associations of America and a member of the Oklahoma State Highway Commission. A federal route requested by Congress was planned to extend from Virginia to Springfield, Missouri, and then farther westward across Kansas, Colorado, Utah, and Nevada into California. Avery, aware that the planned route would not economically benefit his adopted state of Oklahoma, argued for bringing the route south through Oklahoma, Texas, New Mexico, Arizona, and Southern California. His other fateful, and successful, argument was to turn the highway northeast from Springfield, Missouri, through St. Louis to Chicago. Through a compromise, Avery's route, with its diagonal path across Missouri and Illinois, won out and became number 66. In 1927, Avery successfully pushed for the creation of the U.S. Highway 66 Association to promote paving and traveling the new highway.

In 1918, the Illinois State Legislature had authorized the State Bond Issue (SBI) to establish a state highway system. SBI Route 4 was constructed along the old Pontiac Trail and close to the Chicago and Alton Railroad line, connecting the cities of Chicago, Springfield, and St. Louis. In 1926, when Route 66 was designated through Illinois, the paved Illinois Route 4 was the obvious choice to serve as Route 66 until new roads could be built. Illinois was the first state to be able to claim its segment of the new route as paved from border to border.

Frank Thomas Sheets headed the Illinois Division of Highways from 1920 until 1932. Following in the footsteps of his father, Edgar, who was superintendent of the Illinois State Highway Department, Sheets received a degree in highway engineering in 1914 and became assistant maintenance engineer of the Highway Bureau of Maintenance by 1916. Under Sheets's direction, Illinois broke the record four separate times for miles paved in one year by any state. During his tenure, Sheets initiated wider pavements and other highway improvements as well as changes in the path of Route 66.

During the early years of Route 66, horse-drawn vehicles and tractors were still common on the roads and shoulders. The addition of heavy commercial traffic on highways that were common to local and rural use created a sometimes lethal combination. Accidents were common, such as the one that took John Rinkel's life in 1927 on the new Route 66 between Hamel and Edwardsville. Rinkel was driving a team of horses along the shoulder of the highway not far from the family farm when he was struck by a motorized vehicle.

Route 66 was a highway that evolved with the ebb and flow of national and international events. Road construction jobs were some of the few available during the Great Depression of the 1930s. Wartime material shortages in the 1940s halted highway construction. The design and construction elements of the highway evolved as well, reflecting increased traffic, speed, vehicle size, and load weights. Route 66 became wider, thicker, and flatter through the curves as sections of highway were built or rebuilt. Roadside development evolved as well, moving from basic weed cutting and mowing of shoulders to planned landscape improvements and picnic areas.

In 1936, Route 66 was the most heavily traveled road in Illinois. By the end of World War II, Illinois was the top state in the production of armaments, and four-lane sections of highway were necessary near armament factories. Illinois' status as more industrial than some of the other Route 66 states consequently drove the push for stronger highway construction and more lanes. By the 1960s, development of Route 66 was mainly geared for ultimate expansion into the interstate system. In Illinois, Route 66 was in good condition due to rebuilding and was spared a little longer than in other states. Interstate 55 construction began in the late 1950s in Chicago; next on the list was the Metro East/Madison County area, converting the newer four-lane sections to interstate segments.

Madison County's various alignments of Route 66 brought a mixture of travelers through a variety of communities. Traffic was alternately local, long distance, rural, commercial, or recreational. Accidents were numerous, and sightings of Hollywood stars were occasional. The hilly terrain of the bluffs contributed both to the picturesque and pastoral scenery and to the challenges of motoring during the era. Communities near the river shared a more urban, industrial nature and provided a contrast for motorists to the rural villages and farmland that they passed through.

The Hamel to Edwardsville (Route 157) highway was determined in the 1990s by the Illinois Department of Transportation and the Illinois State Historic Preservation Office to be one of only five Route 66 segments in Illinois eligible for the National Register of Historic Places, due to its "integrity of location, design, setting, materials, workmanship, feeling, and association." This approximately 8-mile stretch was constructed expressly for Route 66 in the 1930s.

Route 66 exited Illinois on no less than five different river bridges with nine different bridge names, including the McKinley, the Municipal ("Free," Gen. Douglas MacArthur), the Chain of Rocks, the Veterans' Memorial (Martin Luther King), and the Bernard F. Dickmann (Poplar Street).

One

WORDEN AND HAMEL

John C. Worden founded the coal-mining village of Worden; it was incorporated in 1887. The village of Hamel was named for Andrew Jackson Hamel, a prominent farmer and merchant. Although Hamel was established in the 1800s, it was not incorporated until 1955. In the early 1800s, there were just two roads in what is now Hamel Township: the Kaskaskia and Peoria Trace (later called the Edwardsville-Staunton Road) and a trail from Wood River to Bond County (later called the Alton-Greenville Road, now Illinois Route 140).

Hamel, according to Jack Rittenhouse in his 1946 *A Guidebook to Route 66*, was "a small farming community with several implement stores. Hamel Service Company garage. No cabins or other . . . except gas." Actually, the Tourist Haven Restaurant accommodated travelers with meals and rooms. Today Hamel is a popular spot with Route 66 tourists and tours. Must-sees include Weezy's (formerly the Tourist Haven Restaurant) and the old train station (now Route 66 Beauty and Tanning Salon.)

George Cassens and his family came to this area in the early 1900s. Cassens began selling automobiles and eventually bought property at the main intersection in Hamel, establishing a car dealership, service station, and restaurant. His businesses flourished, and the Cassens family and its success are legend in the Hamel-Edwardsville area. Cassens and his sons began an automobile transport business that revolutionized the manner in which car dealers obtained their inventories. A fire destroyed the service station, but not before the highway was built with a jog to accommodate the business.

Wilton C. Rinkel of the Hamel area was inducted into the Illinois Route 66 Hall of Fame in 1996. He lived his entire life along Route 66 and recalled assisting at numerous accidents and helping stranded motorists along the road between Hamel and Edwardsville. Rinkel farmed and also worked at Cassens Transport, the Hartford Tannery, and Shell Oil Company.

The 1926–1930 alignment of Route 66 brought travelers down Illinois Route 4 past Worden into Hamel. From 1930 on, the route was moved eastward past Livingston to Hamel. Between 1926 and 1955, Route 66 through Hamel was a two-lane highway; it was replaced by four lanes in 1955 and remained so until being decommissioned by the state in 1977.

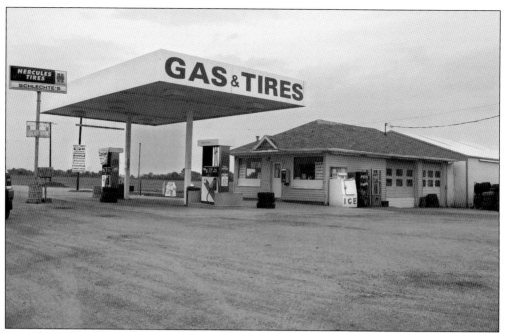

Arvel Schlechte's Service Station has been part of the Worden Y complex for decades. It is located at 7716 State Route 4. This building was built in 1927 by the Schlechte family. When Interstate 55 was constructed just east of this site, the Worden Y buildings were moved a short distance to their present locations. (Photograph by Cheryl Eichar Jett.)

FRANK & HAROLD'S CAFE AND SERVICE STATION
Worden "Y", Illinois — Phone: Hamel 11X36

Frank and Harold's Cafe and Service Station was located at the Worden Y on the older alignment of Route 66. This postcard view shows three sets of gas pumps in front of the café and service station. There is a service bay for automobile work attached to the side of the main building. (Courtesy of Bill Meyer.)

The Worden Y Club was established in the early decades of the 20th century, and a variety of hospitality and automobile service businesses became part of the Worden Y complex. A tavern named Digger's Dugout now occupies the 1927 Worden Y Club building. During the late 1940s through early 1950s, Albert and Martha Suhre managed tourist cabins at the Y. (Photograph by Cheryl Eichar Jett.)

NEARON'S TOURIST CABINS, TRAILER COURT AND TAVERN
On U. S. Highway 66 — Worden, Illinois

Nearon's Tourist Cabins, Trailer Court, and Tavern were located on Route 66 near Worden just south of the Worden Y. This postcard view likely dates from the 1930s. Route 66 runs right in front of the tavern and cabins, with Illinois Terminal railroad tracks behind. (Courtesy of Bill Meyer.)

The blue neon cross on St. Paul Lutheran Church in Hamel still guides travelers after more than 60 years. During World War II, it was placed there by the Brunnworth family in memory of their son who died in Anzio, Italy, in 1944. The redbrick church faced the new four-lane Route 66, which was built in 1955. (Photograph by Peter Stork.)

This Meramec Caverns barn was restored in 2001 by the Illinois Route 66 Association Preservation Committee. It is located near Hamel on the east side of Interstate 55. Lester Dill, who opened the caverns to tourists in 1935 on Route 66 at Stanton, Missouri, thought of a great advertising scheme: Farmers could have their barns painted for free as long as they agreed that Meramec Caverns ads could be part of the paint job. (Photograph by Peter Stork.)

Hamel's Route 66 signs welcome travelers coming into the village from all four directions. Hamel is a popular stop for modern Route 66 tourists. From Hamel, one path of Route 66 headed through Edwardsville and on to Mitchell and the Chain of Rocks Bridge. A later alignment took motorists to Collinsville. (Photograph by Cheryl Eichar Jett.)

Around 1920, when these images were taken, Hamel still had trolley service from Edwardsville. In the image above, the photographer is looking southwest from the intersection of the Alton-Greenville Road (now Route 140) with what would soon be Route 66 stretching away at the left toward Edwardsville. The small, ornate building in front was an early gasoline station. Still standing, the building in the background next to the trolley is now the Route 66 Beauty and Tanning Salon. The photograph below shows a different angle, offering a good view of the two-story building, Cassens's first automobile dealership. Florence Nemnich recalled living as a small child with her family in an apartment in the back of the second floor of this building. Early automobiles and an ornate, crown-topped gasoline pump are visible at the gasoline station. (Both courtesy of Florence Nemnich.)

The Hamel Co-operative Grain Company was founded as a shareholder-owned co-op in March 1920 by a group of area farmers and remains one of Hamel's main businesses. Its primary business is classified as grain and field bean merchant wholesalers with warehousing and storage. (Photograph by Cheryl Eichar Jett.)

The Illinois State Police was founded in 1922. The 52nd General Assembly of the State of Illinois had, in June 1921, authorized the Department of Public Works and Buildings to hire a "sufficient number of State Highway Patrol Officers to enforce the provisions of the Motor Vehicle Laws." This unidentified officer poses in front of the Cassens dealership building in the 1920s. (Courtesy of Karen Wiesemeyer.)

Mechanic Herman "Butch" Reising and two unidentified men stand in front of the Center Garage in the above photograph. The Center Garage did mechanical work for the Cassens auto dealership; the business was located in the former train station. Reising's wife, Anna, worked as a server and dishwasher at the Tourist Haven across Route 66. Cassens Conoco filling station is pictured at left; the station later became known as Hamel Service. The building is still there, although changed in appearance by the addition of siding, and houses the Hamel Car Wash. (Both courtesy of Karen Wiesemeyer.)

From left to right Lester "Butch" Butcher, Wilton C. Rinkel, and Arnold Cassens pose in front of Cassens Used Cars around 1937. Born on the family farm near Hamel in 1915, Rinkel lived his entire life along Route 66 between Hamel and Edwardsville. He died at age 93. At one time, he worked for Cassens Transport. (Courtesy of the Village of Hamel.)

The Wabash Railroad extended into Hamel Township in the 1870s, built a train station in 1877, and also installed a switch northwest of the village. Thousands of bushels of grain were shipped annually, and the population grew. Hamel also enjoyed electric car service for many years. This image shows the station building with the Center Garage business located in it. (Courtesy of Bill Meyer.)

Harold Brunnworth poses in the doorway of his Phillips 66 service station by the sign for Lee Tires. This business was built on Route 66 south of the main intersection, and the property is now the site of the Village of Hamel building. (Courtesy of the Village of Hamel.)

This view of Brunnworth's Phillips 66 service station shows an unidentified employee ready to pump gas for a motorist. In those days, a person really did pump gasoline as opposed to the automatic fuel delivery in use at modern gas stations. The cottage-style station building featured multi-paned windows and shutters with decorative cutouts. (Courtesy of the Village of Hamel.)

This view in Hamel looks north along Route 66 and the Illinois Terminal Railroad tracks. At right is the Tourist Haven Restaurant, which George Cassens had built in the 1930s for his wife, Louise, to operate. At left are Fowley's Tavern, the brick train station, Cassens Conoco service station, and the Hamel Co-op Elevator. Behind the gas station is Cassens automobile dealership. (Courtesy of William A. Raia.)

The Tourist Haven Restaurant was built in the 1930s by George Cassens for his wife, Louise, and since then, has been open for business under various owners and numerous names, including Village Inn, Ernie's, Scotty's, and now Weezy's. It is a popular spot for Route 66 enthusiasts. Travelers can still count on getting a "cold one" and some good diner food at this classic roadside inn. (Photograph by Peter Stork.)

Hamel's pride in its heritage is evident in its preservation and reuse of buildings. Here Sue Minner (right) and her friend Darlene Martin pose on the roof of the old train station. Minner has operated the Route 66 Beauty and Tanning Salon in the building since 2000. (Courtesy of Sue Minner.)

Florence Krejci Gillig remembers growing up on the Krejci family farm near the intersection of Quercus Grove Road and Route 66. The Green Gables Tourist Camp was nearby, across the road from the electric substation. Gillig recalls "heavy, heavy traffic" on Route 66, which caused serious, sometimes fatal, accidents. One collision she remembers involved a motorized vehicle and a team of horses. (Photograph by Cheryl Eichar Jett.)

Klueter Brothers Concrete Products at 5757 North State Route 157 has long been a landmark along Route 66 between Hamel and Edwardsville. Brothers Virgil and LeRoy established the Klueter Brothers business in 1947, and the plant remains on the same site. The first products the company manufactured were septic tanks. In 1982, Virgil and LeRoy retired and sold the company to Rich Krumm and Donald Posey from Missouri. (Photograph by Cheryl Eichar Jett.)

Eileen Sedlacek is getting her kicks on Route 66, even if her feet hurt. In preparation for a Route 66 festival in Edwardsville, Roy and Edna Wolfe unearthed this photograph of Edna's sister Eileen. The picture was taken in the 1940s near Edwardsville. (Courtesy of the City of Edwardsville.)

Two

WILLIAMSON AND LIVINGSTON

Williamson and Livingston are adjacent rural villages in northern Madison County surrounded by farmland and coal mines. Livingston, a community dependent primarily on local coal mines for employment, was incorporated in 1905 and named for the Livingston family, on whose property the village was laid out. The New Staunton Coal Company was established about the same time, virtually creating the village of mine employees. Loads of lumber from the demolished buildings of the St. Louis World's Fair were used to build many of the first houses. In 1930, the New Staunton Coal Company closed, but two years later, the Livingston–Mount Olive Coal Company opened.

In 1940, the realignment of Route 66 was built around the southeast corner of Livingston, bringing travelers through the edge of the community. Livingston was located on the path of Route 66 from 1940 through 1977, and motorists could drive directly onto Livingston Avenue. After Interstate 55 was constructed, access to Livingston was moved a quarter mile away via Exit 37. This exit still brings travelers along the frontage road parallel to the interstate.

According to Jack DeVere Rittenhouse in his 1946 *A Guide Book to Highway 66*, "US 66 barely touches the eastern edge of Livingston (population 1,115). Gas station on highway." Actually, Livingston offered not only the Standard Oil service station along Route 66, but also a repair garage and a café. There were also gas pumps at the Livingston Cooperative Store, Mitchelar Hardware, Bike's Garage, Busker's Store, Dave Bononi's gas station, and Warlock's. The Livingston Community High School, constructed in 1926, was right next to Route 66 and just across from the Standard Oil station; the last class graduated in 2004. Many baby boomers remember the KenDon Restaurant, which was also situated on Route 66 and later destroyed by fire.

Today travelers and locals alike shop at the Pink Elephant Antique Mall, which fits interestingly into the old high school's spaces. In front of the antique mall, an assortment of small structures including an ice-cream-cone-shaped ice cream stand and a UFO attract the traveler's eye.

One of the first sights travelers may have seen after crossing into Madison County in the late 1940s or 1950s was the W. L. S. Airport, named for the nearby towns of Williamson, Livingston, Staunton. Five men—Elmer France, Arthur "Bike" Coalson, and John Repovsch from Livingston; Ted Dworzynski of Staunton; and Lt. John Bellovich of Williamson—established W. L. S. Airport on 80 acres of Repovsch's land near the Route 66 overpass above the Big Four Railroad. In its first year, the airport had four airplanes available for passenger service. (Courtesy of the Livingston Centennial Committee.)

In 1936, Joe Sandrin built this Standard Oil service station in Livingston. Eventually Joe's son Elmer took over the establishment and, in the 1950s, closed this location and demolished the building. He moved the business across the street, reopening as two more highway lanes were being built. Despite the new building, Elmer lost interest in the business and became a teacher. Management of the station passed to Robert "Doc" Bowles and Richard Meyer. (Courtesy of the Livingston Centennial Committee.)

In front of Joe Sandrin's Standard Oil service station, from left to right, Elmer "Beb" Sandrin, Emil Libbra, and "Fat" Stanko pose on car. This service station was built in the house with canopy architectural style typical of many early stations. (Courtesy of the Livingston Centennial Committee.)

Robert "Doc" Bowles and Richard Meyer opened the Bowles and Meyer Standard Oil service station in April 1956 on Livingston Avenue. This location was just east of the high school and consequently was a popular hangout for Livingston teenagers. During the 19 years that Bowles and Meyer operated the station, approximately 50 high school boys, including two of Richard's sons and Doc's son, worked there. Doc's dad, Levi "Red" Bowles, and his uncle, Ira Bowles Sr., also worked at the station. Its accessibility to Route 66 in addition to local customers ensured success. When Interstate 55 was constructed nearby, the highway entrance to Livingston Avenue was closed, and a new entrance via an overpass was constructed a quarter mile away. The station soon closed. (Both courtesy of the Livingston Centennial Committee.)

After the Bowles and Meyer Station closed, Richard Meyer purchased a parcel of land at Exit 37 on Interstate 55 from the Amoco Oil Company. In 1976, he opened a new, modern gas station and food mart. This image shows the station today. (Photograph by Miles Dudley.)

If a traveler needed car repair while in the Livingston area, there was a garage not far from Route 66 on South First Street. Arthur "Bike" Coalson Sr. began his repair business in the 1920s and by the early 1930s built this garage and station. After World War II, Bike's son Arthur Jr. "Gejo" joined his father in the business. In 1987, Larry Bernardin bought the business but closed it two years later. (Courtesy of the Livingston Centennial Committee.)

Owned by shareholders, Livingston Cooperative Store was opened on Livingston Avenue by the United Mine Workers of America. Workers and their families could purchase groceries, clothing, shoes, appliances, and household needs there. As the community prospered, a larger store was built at the corner of Livingston Avenue and South First Street. Gasoline was also available, as shown in this 1928 photograph. (Courtesy of the Livingston Centennial Committee.)

This photograph shows the Kendon Restaurant the day it was destroyed by fire. Kenny and Don Ackerman were the final owners of the restaurant, where they had added a motel and expanded the café. Previous operators at this location were Ann Scheibe, with Scheibe's Café; Elmer "Beb" Sandrin, with Sandrin's Café; and Adolph and Shirley Hebenstreit, operating Fud's Café. (Courtesy of the Livingston Centennial Committee.)

Ann Scheibe of Edwardsville poses with her brother Walter Rademacher and young Tom (left) and Bob Wetzel in the early 1940s. During the late 1940s and early 1950s, Ann operated Scheibe's Café in Livingston, which eventually became the Kendon Restaurant. Joe's Auto Repair now occupies the former restaurant site. (Courtesy of the City of Edwardsville.)

Livingston Community High School was constructed in 1926 on Livingston Avenue. The 1940–1977 alignment of Route 66 went right by the high school. The last senior class graduated in 2004, prior to the school's consolidation into the nearby Staunton school district. The redbrick building now houses the Pink Elephant Antique Mall. Travelers, tourists, and locals stop to check out the booths. (Photograph by Miles Dudley.)

In 2000, Historic Route 66 signs were placed along Livingston's west frontage route to indicate the 1940–1977 path as it passed through the southeastern part of town. Although the Illinois Department of Transportation began to place signs designating the highway in 1995, this stretch of the 1940–1977 roadway went unmarked at the time. The persistence of Anne Perne Gregor, Livingston citizens, and the village board resulted in the erection of the signs. (Photograph by Miles Dudley.)

Three

EDWARDSVILLE

Edwardsville was founded over 200 years ago when settler Thomas Kirkpatrick built a cabin on land above Cahokia Creek, not far from what is now North Main Street. Kirkpatrick's friend Ninian Edwards, appointed territorial governor in 1809, designated Kirkpatrick's cabin as the county seat of Madison County. Kirkpatrick named the new town Edwardsville. Fort Russell, a military blockhouse, was constructed to the northwest. By 1820, the town was platted, stores had opened, and a U.S. land grant office and an Indian agency were in place. Edwardsville has served as the seat of law and government for Madison County ever since. It also became an agricultural center of trade and acquired several industries, including grain mills, coal mines, and brickyards. The city is situated in a hilly area just east of the floodplain known as the American Bottom.

Route 66 (now known as State Route 157) stretched from Hamel to Edwardsville, up Mooney Hill on Hillsboro Road, and through the downtown area on Vandalia Street. The route alternately followed Hillsboro Avenue down to Main Street and then to Vandalia Street. From there, St. Louis Street, West Street, and St. Louis Road completed the route through Edwardsville down onto Chain of Rocks Road. Older residents remember the heavy traffic.

Along the route, motorists identified Edwardsville's landmarks, such as the Carnegie Library and the Centennial Monument along the Vandalia Street path. A variety of cafés, taverns, and lodgings lined the route. Servers and store clerks remember some well-known entertainers stopping in Edwardsville, including television and film actor Danny Thomas and popular singers Ferlin Husky and Brenda Lee.

Edwardsville has celebrated its Route 66 heritage with Route 66 festivals since the 1990s. The city, besides its long history as the county seat, is the home of Southern Illinois University Edwardsville (SIUE) and, more recently, Lewis and Clark Community College, in the historic N. O. Nelson complex. Three historic districts—Leclaire, the St. Louis Street District, and the Brick Street District—attest to the city's interest in historic preservation. On Saturday mornings from May through October, the Goshen Farmers and Community Market preserves the tradition of selling local agricultural and artistic products.

A storm hit the Edwardsville area on September 30, 1940, and downed utility poles. Traffic appears to be proceeding cautiously. (Photograph by John Cocker; courtesy of the City of Edwardsville.)

The steep grade of Mooney Hill let motorists know they were approaching Edwardsville. In this image, lines for counting traffic are faintly visible across the highway. Delmar Schoenleber, a longtime Route 66 resident, recalled the winter of 1941, when "a three-truck accident blocked traffic for 12 hours. One truck stalled and another tried to pass him, but a third truck coming from the other direction could not stop, and a gas tank exploded." (Courtesy of the City of Edwardsville.)

This photograph shows The Alibi at Mooney Hill (4500 State Route 157). In 1946, after returning home from World War II, carpenter Lester Gebhart and his father, Joe, built the tavern and restaurant. The Gebhart family ran the business and lived next door; Joe mowed the grass along Route 66 with a team of mules and a mower. In front of the door are Peg (dark-colored shirt) and Elda Crook. (Courtesy of the City of Edwardsville.)

Ann Scheibe, who managed several different restaurants over the years, is pictured here in the 1940s with Ray Cabello. Ann and Ray ran the Gebhart family's Alibi tavern and restaurant for a number of years, calling it the Ray Ann Café. There was a large parking lot, and truckers would use it as a turnaround. (Courtesy of the City of Edwardsville.)

In 1941, the owner, Mr. Bartlett, leased 931 Hillsboro Avenue to Tillie Francisconi and Helen Zahradka. They opened the White Kitchen Restaurant and, years later, recalled the hard work. "We opened at 6:00 a.m., and sometimes we didn't get home until 4:00 a.m. the following day," Francisconi remembered. Her brother Clarence Hoppe lived across the street and watched the road crew pave Route 66 with bricks. (Courtesy of the City of Edwardsville.)

Jackson Service Station at 927 Hillsboro Avenue was next to the White Kitchen. Truckers would reportedly increase the weight of cattle loads headed for the slaughterhouses in East St. Louis by adding water from the station, and the smell of wet farm animals would waft from trucks traveling down Hillsboro Avenue through downtown Edwardsville. (Courtesy of the City of Edwardsville.)

Halley's Market was the first grocery store that travelers came upon when entering Edwardsville. When the highway was first designated as Route 66, Costas Coroniotis was operating the Superior Cash and Carry Grocery at this location. In 1927, Thomas and Mayme Halley purchased the building and business and operated it as Halley's Cash Market until 1972. The store carried canned goods, cereal, dairy products, candy, snacks, and comic books. This 1970s photograph shows Hazel's Re-Sell It shop in the building; owners John and Hazel Hemmerle bought it from the Halleys in 1970 and left the "Halley's" Sign in place. Springer's Creek Winery now occupies the building. (Courtesy of the Madison County Historical Society.)

This beautifully restored home at 732 Hillsboro Road was the Merle Lawder Tourist Home from 1950 to 1978. Merle rented out rooms for $1 a night, while she slept upstairs in the attic. Some nights, 30 to 35 people would be sleeping on the floor. One of the famous Gabor sisters is said to have stayed there. The beautiful Italianate home is known as the Happy House, since it was built for attorney Cyrus Happy around 1880. (Courtesy of the City of Edwardsville.)

Hillsboro Avenue, as it turned west toward downtown Edwardsville, was also Route 66 for a period of time. After the turn, the street was residential for several blocks. Closer to downtown on Hillsboro Avenue stood the post office and the Masonic Temple. (Courtesy of June Nealy.)

Oliver and Norma Jacober built Jacober's Market at 141 St. Andrews Avenue in 1947 and operated it for the next 25 years. Oliver remembered a variety of customers that came in off the busy highway. During beet-harvesting season, many immigrant workers would stop in for food. One day, actor Danny Thomas walked in and bought chewing tobacco and also left money for treats for all the children in the store. (Courtesy of City of Edwardsville.)

The Site Service Station near Jacober's Market was opened in 1939 by twin brothers Hubert and Jerry Keshner. Later operators of the filling station included Blackie Hogue and Dallas Harold. Blackie's son Charlie worked the midnight shift, and night policeman Charlie Kreeger would pull in to the station and help pass the time on a slow night. Roy Wolfe was driving a taxi at that time and remembered buying gas there for 10¢ a gallon. (Courtesy of City of Edwardsville.)

Supported by federal money, the Madison Construction Company repaved Route 66 through Edwardsville in 1938 and 1939. In this view, the company's pavement pulverizer, a large jackhammer of the company's own design, operates just west of the East Vandalia Street railroad tracks. The jackhammer could strike 60 to 70 blows per minute, smashing the old brick paving and the concrete foundation underneath. Besides rebuilding Route 66 through the city, other local New Deal projects included removing abandoned electric railroad tracks and resurfacing the center of the city's streets, and building the Edwardsville–Wood River Road. (Courtesy of the Madison County Historical Society.)

Route 66 was being repaved in the late 1930s when these photographs were taken. This building at 463 East Vandalia Street dates from about 1918, and Frank and Dorothy Catalano operated the Hi-Way Tavern here for many years. In the late 1940s, when Cathcart's Café across the street added a bar, Catalano decided to add a restaurant to his Hi-Way Tavern. He owned the house next door and rented it to George and Mary Lautner. He built the café on the front of the house. Eventually the Lautners took over the operation and ran it from 1947 until 1960. The Lautners were open 12 hours a day, with Mary serving as the day cook and George cooking in the evenings. They continued to live in the house behind the restaurant. (Both courtesy of the City of Edwardsville.)

This shot shows the interior of the Hi-Way Café about 1950. Behind the counter are Gwen Evans (Eberhart) and an unidentified milkman making a delivery. The customer is also unidentified. George and Mary Lautner remembered baking 24 pies every day. The Lautners recalled a wide variety of customers: bus loads of school children, local plant workers, Chicago Cubs fans, and even the Budweiser Clydesdales (with their driver). (Courtesy of City of Edwardsville.)

Ruth King Schramek worked as a waitress at Cathcart's Café in the 1940s for 50¢ to 75¢ an hour. "Mousie" was her nickname because she could "whiz through the crowds and find a hole" to get to her orders. Schramek remembered busloads coming in after high school games. She worked at the café from the time she was 15 until she got married at age 33 to John Schramek, whom she met at Cathcart's. (Courtesy of the City of Edwardsville.)

George Cathcart opened Cathcart's Café across the street from the Hi-Way Tavern in the 1920s. It was a popular hangout for local customers, especially teenagers, and was also billed as "famous from coast to coast" for home-cooked meals, tourist information, and groceries. Cathcart's was open 24 hours a day to serve customers around the clock. The parking lot between the café and the house next door served as the Greyhound bus terminal. (Courtesy of June Nealy.)

This crowd was typical of Friday and Saturday nights after high school games, when students and parents crammed into Cathcart's Café. Ruth King Schramek, a server there in her teens, remembered the jukebox playing, the packed tables, and the wild teenagers. "If you'd turn the volume down on the jukebox, they'd turn it back up! They'd turn their full water glasses over and I'd have to figure out how to clear the table," Ruth recalled. (Courtesy of the City of Edwardsville.)

The Fred Goddard family lived in this home from 1931 to 1978 and operated Goddard's Tourist Home from 1932 to 1954. There were rooms upstairs and several cabins on the property. Joanna Goddard Watson remembered, "If the light was on, people would know that there was a room. Nobody even thought about breaking in. Our door was open most every night." (Courtesy of the City of Edwardsville.)

At the Goddard Tourist Home, there was also a larger cottage available for longer stays. While Dr. Maurice Sanderson, who lived in the cottage, and his new bride, Elizabeth, were away on their honeymoon, Fred Goddard decided to expand the cottage. It was raised with jacks and a new lower level was built underneath it. When the tourist business fell off, Goddard tore down the three original tourist cabins and reused the lumber to build a three-room rental cottage, which is still there. (Courtesy of the City of Edwardsville.)

This June 1947 image shows newlyweds Maurice and Elizabeth Sanderson. Elizabeth had moved to Edwardsville a year earlier from Waco, Texas, and met Dr. Sanderson when she moved into the Goddard Tourist Home. A decade later, Dr. Sanderson was shot and killed by an intruder in their house on Home Avenue. (Courtesy of the City of Edwardsville.)

In October 1931, John Fischer and his son Erwin drove from Edwardsville to California and back on Route 66, putting 6,500 miles on their Ford Model T. The trip was a father-and-son adventure they decided to go on together. Here Fischer's sister-in-law Barbara Fischer (right) and his daughter Agnes Fischer Halbe welcome the adventurers back home. They are posed in front of the trusty Ford after the men's return trip. (Courtesy of Michele Fischer Stark.)

Young Erwin Fischer poses in the Model T after returning from the Route 66 road trip with his father. John Fischer built two family homes on Sherman Street at the edge of Leclaire. Erwin's granddaughter Michele Fischer Stark noted that "Grandpa would have loved" having their photographs and story included in a book about Route 66. (Courtesy of Michele Fischer Stark.)

St. Boniface Catholic Church was built in 1869 at the corner of Buchanan and Vandalia Streets by H. Melcher's construction company of St. Louis from a plan submitted by A. Druiding, also of St. Louis. Rev. William Kuchenbuch had purchased 20 lots on that corner a few years earlier. The church was constructed on the site of the former home of Ninian Edwards, Illinois territorial governor and Edwardsville's namesake. (Courtesy of Neal Strebel.)

The Texaco station at the corner of Vandalia and Buchanan Streets was operated first by Sparky Meyer, next by Chester and Paul Michel, and then, by the time of this image, by George Weiler and his sons Terry and Bob. Bob Weiler remembers pumping gas for country-western singer Ferlin Husky when he pulled into the station. After Route 66 was rerouted, Bob was continually answering tourists' questions about the location of the highway. (Courtesy of the City of Edwardsville.)

Earl Orman owned the Standard Oil franchise at 201 East Vandalia Street from 1934 to 1966. Orman's daughter Erlene remembered that it started out as a "teeny, tiny station." Seen here in the 1930s, it was built in the house with canopy architectural style typical of gasoline stations of that era. Through their high school and college years, Orman's daughters Beverly and Erlene worked at the station, waiting on cars and pumping gas. (Courtesy of the City of Edwardsville.)

The *Narodni Sin*, which means "national hall" in Czech, was built on Vandalia Street in 1906 by Anton Hlad. The letters CCPS stand for *Cecho Slovensky Podporujici Spolky*, or Czechoslovak Protective Society. On the first floor of the structure in 1910, the Park Saloon offered "wines, liquors and cigars" and "Louis Obert Brew." The building is on the National Register of Historic Places. (Courtesy of Neal Strebel.)

The Edwardsville Public Library, located in City Park, was right on Route 66. In 1903, Charles Boeschenstein, Edwardsville mayor and publisher of the *Intelligencer*, wrote to Andrew Carnegie requesting funds for a public library. Carnegie responded with a $12,500 check. The city of Edwardsville donated land in City Park. (Courtesy of June Nealy.)

The Madison County Centennial monument was commissioned as an outdoor sculpture to be placed in City Park in 1912 as a lasting reminder of the centennial. Made of Georgia marble on a stone base, it measures approximately 15 feet high by 6 feet square. One of the inscriptions reads, "Commemorating a century of achievement." The sculptor was Charles J. Mulligan. (Courtesy of June Nealy.)

This World War II Roll of Honor sign was erected in City Park along Vandalia Street/Route 66. There are 975 Edwardsville residents' names listed in this 1946 photograph. A similar sign had been put up at the courthouse years before to honor those who served in World War I. (Courtesy of the Madison County Historical Society.)

The Edwardsville Creamery Company (ECCO) building at Park and Johnson Streets (just behind the library and City Park) was brand new when Route 66 began to bring travelers through Edwardsville. Martin Jensen founded the company in 1927 and remained at that address for half a century. If travelers purchased dairy products at one of the local grocery stores, they were likely buying Edwardsville Creamery products. (Courtesy of the Madison County Historical Society.)

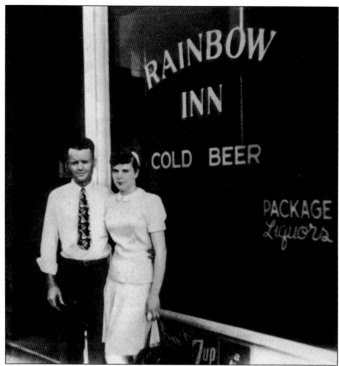

Peg and Elda Crook pose in front of the Rainbow Inn around 1947. Today this is the Stagger Inn Again, known for its live music, open-mike nights, food, and mixture of age groups. The Stagger Inn Again celebrated its 25th anniversary and the 36th anniversary of the original Stagger Inn in July 2010. (Courtesy of the City of Edwardsville.)

The Kriege name has been associated with hardware in Edwardsville since the 1880s, and Kriege Hardware has been at this location on Vandalia Street since the 1940s. It is the last hardware store in town with a local family name. The Solter family, as seen on the sign, co-owned the hardware store at one time. (Courtesy of the City of Edwardsville.)

The Bohm Building at the corner of Main and Vandalia (Route 66) Streets is an Edwardsville landmark. It was built in 1910 by William Bohm, a farmer and local businessman, and the building served as Edwardsville's first office building. The third floor was added later to provide a ballroom for Bohm's son Clarence to give ballroom dance lessons in. Clarence had attended ballroom dance school in California and was eager to share his prowess. (Courtesy of June Nealy.)

A hometown parade marches south on Vandalia Street/Route 66 in 1946. At left is May's Rexall Drugs, which was located in the Bohm Building. In the right-hand block are Yonaka Jewelry and the Rainbo Inn, later known as Stagger Inn. In 1936, Hollywood cowboy actor Tom Mix and his wife were spotted driving through this intersection on Route 66. (Courtesy of the City of Edwardsville.)

At the intersection of Vandalia Street/Route 66 with Edwardsville's Main Street, a Route 66 sign directs travelers straight ahead toward St. Louis. The driver in the car in front of Ballweg Drugs at right is unidentified. A newer brick office building now occupies that entire block, and a Walgreens sits on the corner across the street, where the DeSoto dealership and Deep Rock Service Station stood. (Courtesy of the Madison County Historical Society.)

A c. 1940 aerial view of downtown Edwardsville shows Route 66 (Vandalia Street) slicing through town near the middle of the image. At a diagonal from Vandalia Street, Main Street runs northwest between the courthouse (upper left center) and downtown stores. (Photograph by Aero-Graphic Corporation; courtesy of the City of Edwardsville.)

The U.S. Postal Service building, with its octagonal tower entrance, opened at the intersection of Hillsboro and Commercial Streets in 1915. At that time, T. M. Crossman was the postmaster and W. M. Crossman Sr. was the assistant postmaster. Postmaster Crossman's salary was around $2,500 per year. Although no longer used as the post office, the building still stands. (Courtesy of June Nealy.)

The Masonic Temple was constructed in 1927 on Hillsboro Avenue for Masonic Lodge No. 99, which received its charter in 1851. There were about 300 members at the time. The building is still standing. (Courtesy of June Nealy.)

If travelers ventured just a couple blocks off Route 66, they might have stopped for a movie at the Wildey Theatre on Main Street. The Wildey was constructed as part of the Independent Order of Odd Fellows (IOOF) Lodge in 1909. A veritable who's who of big-name entertainment played there in the early days, including W. C. Fields, Al Jolson, and Ginger Rogers. Movies were shown up until 1984. The City of Edwardsville acquired the property in 1999 and has completed exterior renovations. (Courtesy of June Nealy.)

Arriving at the intersection of Hillsboro Avenue and Main Street in Edwardsville, Route 66 travelers could see the five-story Bank of Edwardsville, the city's first "skyscraper." Edward M. West and his son-in-law Maj. William R. Prickett founded West and Prickett, later renamed the Bank of Edwardsville, on January 1, 1868. The building in this photograph was built in the 1910s and demolished in 1990. (Courtesy of June Nealy.)

This promotional steam engine on tires was designed to promote interest in working for the railroads. With the end of the war in sight, more workers would be needed to handle material and returning troops. In this photograph, the engine is parked on North Main Street in front of the courthouse. Across the street is Woolworth's, a popular stop for Route 66 travelers needing supplies. (Courtesy of the Madison County Historical Society.)

Covering almost an entire city block, Edwardsville's fourth and present courthouse has an exterior of unpolished white Georgia marble. Its dedication on October 18, 1915, drew a huge crowd. The architect was Robert G. Kirsch of St. Louis, who also designed the Miners' Theatre in nearby Collinsville. (Courtesy of June Nealy.)

The National Recovery Administration (NRA) parade on October 20, 1933, demonstrated, according to the *Edwardsville Intelligencer*, "the city's willingness to co-operate in the national business recovery program." A 21-foot-by-30-foot banner with the NRA Blue Eagle thunderbird symbol is carried by 21 newsboys. The parade is said to have taken 47 minutes to pass any given point. (Courtesy of the Madison County Historical Society.)

In 1923, the Edwardsville National Bank joined the Bank of Edwardsville as another modern building flanking the courthouse. The large clock on the corner of this five-story building made it very recognizable. Although the old Edwardsville National Bank building is long gone, the clock was preserved and later mounted on a brick tower in the 200 block of North Main Street. (Courtesy of June Nealy.)

60

An unusual sight on Edwardsville's Main Street was this Japanese submarine on display on August 19, 1943. The captured, two-man submarine was being used to promote the purchase of war bonds. After being studied by U.S. naval engineers, the 81-foot submarine was sent out on a special truck for fund-raising duties. A large crowd gathered to inspect the submarine, which originally carried two torpedoes and sufficient explosives to blow it up after the torpedoes had been fired. (Courtesy of the Madison County Historical Society.)

This photograph, taken before 1964, shows Edwardsville's Main Street looking northwest from near the intersection with Vandalia Street/Route 66. At left are the Edwardsville National Bank with its large clock, the county courthouse, and the Bank of Edwardsville. On the right side of the street are Ballweg Drugs and a variety of retail businesses. (Courtesy of June Nealy.)

The Palace Store anchored the west side of Main Street in the 100 block for most of the 20th century. The 1912 *History of Madison County* claims it to be "the largest mercantile establishment at Edwardsville." The building was demolished in 1988, and Southern Illinois University Edwardsville rescued some of the terra-cotta architectural ornaments. (Courtesy of June Nealy.)

Heidelberg Oil Company was located at 100 West Vandalia Street. This *c.* 1936 photograph shows owner Roland Heidelberg next to his sign advertising gas prices; note the 16¢ economy gas. Heidelberg's station was a Deep Rock Service Station. A later station owner was Bill Mindrup. (Courtesy of the City of Edwardsville.)

Butler Chevrolet was established at 120 West Vandalia Street in 1928 by Harry Butler. This photograph taken in the early 1940s showing the "Buy Used Cars 1936–1942" sign is a reminder of hard times during the World War II years. Fuel, oil, and tires were rationed and were hard to come by. Local men who worked as mechanics went off to war. (Courtesy of the City of Edwardsville.)

The Butler Chevrolet showroom had a neon Chevrolet sign in the window and a checkerboard tile floor. A Butler family member identified the customer holding a small child as Charles Vieth. After World War II, there was a huge demand for new cars. People were beginning to head from Chicago to the Southwest and often needed service on their vehicles about the time they reached Edwardsville. (Courtesy of the City of Edwardsville.)

Frances Butler poses with a Chevrolet woody wagon in the 1940s in front of Butler Chevrolet. The building behind her belonged to veterinarian Louis J. Stortz, from whom the Butlers purchased the property for their car dealership (Courtesy of the City of Edwardsville.)

Robert Wadlow, known as the "Gentle Giant," was born in 1918 in Alton to average-sized parents. The friendly but shy Wadlow grew to be the world's tallest man at a height of 8 feet, 11 inches. He toured with Ringling Brothers Circus and, as a popular American celebrity, made personal appearances. Here he is shown at Butler Chevrolet with Harry Butler. Wadlow died at age 22, and more than 40,000 people attended his funeral. (Courtesy of the City of Edwardsville.)

In 1954, Quade's 66 Service opened at 141 West Vandalia Street, with young Jack Minner working alongside Bill Quade. In 1960, Minner and Jack Gerhardt purchased the business, calling it Jacks' Service. Minner bought out Gerhardt in 1965 and ran Jacks' 66 until 1998, when he moved to another location. Minner figures it was the last operating business on Route 66 in Edwardsville to close. (Courtesy of the City of Edwardsville.)

The A&B Feed and Seed Store, Inc. at 145 West Vandalia Street, across the street from Butler Chevrolet, burned in the early 1940s. Bundled in coats and hats, a large crowd of people gathered to watch the fire department work tirelessly to control the blaze. (Courtesy of the Madison County Historical Society.)

Albert Bothman established the Albert Bothman and Sons Ford dealership (above) at 306 West Vandalia Street in 1921. Bothman also apparently sold tractors and tractor-drawn farm machinery at one time. A September 22, 1921, article in the *Columbia Evening Missourian* states that Bothman "will launch a plan to interest farmers in using tractors and tractor-drawn machinery in cultivating farms. He has leased a 60-acre farm at Edwardsville, where there will be daily demonstrations in the preparations of soil for planting wheat." Albert Bothman and Sons Ford employees line up for an early picture in front of the service garage (below). (Both courtesy of the City of Edwardsville.)

The Edwardsville Hotel at the corner of Benton and West Vandalia Streets featured a coffee shop. In 1929, William M. Zentgraf was the proprietor; he and his wife, Nettie, were listed in the 1929 city directory as living at the hotel. Ruth L. Zentgraf, their daughter, was the cashier. (Courtesy of the City of Edwardsville.)

Orville West used the former location of the A. O. French residence at the corner of St. Louis and Myrtle Streets to sell popcorn, hot dogs, tamales, and root beer from this wagon. In the 1950s, the Kaufmanns would build an A&W Drive-In there. (Courtesy of the City of Edwardsville.)

In 1954, Mel and Vonney Kaufmann moved from Wisconsin to begin an A&W Drive-In on a piece of land they had purchased at the corner of St. Louis and Myrtle Streets. Vonney's sister and brother-in-law operated an A&W in Springfield at that time, and the Kaufmanns were encouraged by the Springfield eatery's success. Temperatures of up to 114 degrees that summer, high humidity, no air-conditioning in the new building, and controversy over the commercial enterprise starting up on the old residential street did not give the Kaufmanns an easy start. They worked 14-hour days, seven days a week. (Both courtesy of Michael A. and Carol Sporrer.)

The Kaufmanns prospered, and A&W became an institution in Edwardsville. The biggest crowds were after performances at the Mississippi River Festival at Southern Illinois University Edwardsville (SIUE) from 1969 to 1980. In the 1960s and 1970s, the A&W was owned and operated by the Kaufmann's son Dennis and his wife, Carol. In 1977, the same year Dennis was killed in a car accident, scenes for the movie *Stingray* were filmed at the A&W. Carol married Michael Sporrer in 1980, and they hired a business manager. Sandy McNeil (Dennis Kaufmann's stepsister) and her husband, Art, bought the franchise in 1990, but it closed for good in 2000. The building has since been torn down. (Both courtesy of Michael A. and Carol Sporrer.)

The West End Service Station, with Mobilgas lights on the pumps, was located at 620 St. Louis Street, where Route 66 turned left onto West Street. In this photograph, the 1940 Edwardsville High School homecoming parade marches around the corner. After 44 years as a service station, the brick building was converted into a dental office in 1966. (Courtesy of the Madison County Historical Society.)

Christmas decorations are being installed on the roof of the West End Service Station, owned by Hank Dohle and Doc Heidinger in the 1950s. Bill Kleffman recalled working there for $1 an hour performing maintenance on valves and piston rings. The station had a single island of pumps, one car wash bay, and one service bay. (Courtesy of the Madison County Historical Society.)

From left to right, Mary Simons, Eileen Kleuter, and Virginia Abendroth pose for a snapshot in 1938 at the West End Service Station. Just a block away from the new Edwardsville High School, the station was a hangout for teenagers buying sodas or, as Steve Ellsworth remembered, was "kind of a loafing place for seniors." (Courtesy of Steve Rezabek.)

This retaining wall at the edge of the Hadley property was known as a great perch for high school students to relax after a day of classes and watch the traffic go by on Route 66. Mary Barnsback Byron recalled counting out-of-state license plates here on summer nights. In this image, a photographer uses it to get a better view of the passing parade. (Courtesy of the Madison County Historical Society.)

The Hadley House at the corner of St. Louis and West Streets, where Route 66 made a left turn, was built in 1875 as a wedding gift to W. F. L. and Mary Hadley from Mary's parents, Edward and Julia West. W. F. L. served as an Illinois state senator. In 1953, the mansion was acquired by the Edwardsville Community School District and has since then served as the district's central office. (Courtesy of the City of Edwardsville.)

The main building of the new Edwardsville High School was completed in 1925 on acreage between St. Louis and Schwarz Streets. The gymnasium was not added until 1928 because of a lack of funds. The architect of the three-story edifice was M. B. Kane, one of several generations of Edwardsville architects. Route 66 curved right around the high school, giving rise to traffic watching and traffic guessing games among students looking out the windows. (Courtesy of June Nealy.)

Frank and Mildred Hesler owned and operated this Standard Oil service station and small café on Route 66 past the new Edwardsville High School. The architectural style of this early gas station is house with canopy, with the café section added on to the side. (Courtesy of the City of Edwardsville.)

Orval and Virginia Legate bought 12 acres of land from Frank Spindler and built Legate's Motel in 1948. Mel Suhre was the contractor of the 19-unit lodging. Genieve Miller was the clerk and continued to live on Legate's Curve long after the lodging was torn down. M. L. Mixon served as the housekeeper during the motel's 16 years of business. Orval Legate bought a truck from the Cassens auto dealership to haul water for motel use. (Courtesy of June Nealy.)

Legate's Motel had a trailer park with three rows of mobile homes behind the restaurant. Construction workers from Shell and Standard service stations, Southern Illinois University, and the Chain of Rocks Bridge stayed in the trailer park. There was a separate bathhouse and a large laundry room with wringer washers. Orval Legate served as the motel handyman. (Courtesy of the City of Edwardsville.)

On Legate's Curve next to Legate's Motel sat the Hilltop House Restaurant. A pig, chicken, and cow made out of plywood decorated the facade of the eatery. Fried chicken, steaks, open-faced beef sandwiches, and spaghetti, plus homemade pie made by Maria Moss were some of the specialties. Patrons remembered sitting in one of the booths up front by the big picture windows, and it "looked like people were going to come right at you on that curve." (Courtesy of the City of Edwardsville.)

The Edward Coles monument was erected in Valley View Cemetery by the State of Illinois in 1928. A quote by Coles, an anti-slavery Illinois governor, is inscribed on the monument: "Believing slavery to be both injurious and impolitic, I believe myself bound, both as a citizen and an officer, to do all in my power to prevent its introduction into the state." (Courtesy of the Madison County Historical Society.)

Southern Illinois University Edwardsville (SIUE) opened in 1964 as a commuter school on 2,600 acres of rolling ground atop the Mississippi River bluffs. The core campus was constructed on the site of the Freund family farm. Gyo Obata, of the St. Louis firm Hellmuth, Obata, and Casaba, was the architect; Obata also designed the James S. McDonnell Planetarium at the St. Louis Science Center. (Courtesy of SJ Morrison.)

The Mississippi River Festival was held from 1969 through 1980 in a natural amphitheater on the rolling land of the SIUE campus with a huge tent at the bottom to cover the stage, performers, and approximately 1,800 seats. It was designed to provide a stage view to another 8,000 outside the tent. As many as 30,000 music fans attended some concerts. The St. Louis Symphony, Judy Collins, and Bob Dylan and the Band were some of the featured performers. (Courtesy of June Nealy.)

The Home Nursery south of Edwardsville on Route 66 was built by Ernest Tosovsky Sr. and operated by Tosovsky and his two partners, Joe Foulech and Ed Burns. Foulech eventually left to start Sunnyside Nursery in Troy, and Burns ventured out on his own to establish the Burns Nursery. A lot of traffic past the business brought in customers. (Courtesy of the City of Edwardsville.)

The E. G. Golf Club was established in 1922, with the first nine holes designed in 1924 by Larry Packard. In the 1950s, Packard and Brent Wadsworth worked together on laying out the original back nine. Also during that decade, the name was changed to Sunset Hills Country Club. It is one of the oldest golf clubs in southern Illinois and considered to still be steeped in tradition. (Courtesy of Neal Strebel.)

The Edwardsville Holiday Inn is perhaps best remembered for singer Jackson Browne recording two songs there for his album *Running on Empty*. In August 1977, Tracks A5, "Cocaine," and B1, "Shaky Town," were recorded in room 124. The site at 3080 South Route 157 is now a Comfort Inn. (Courtesy of June Nealy.)

Anne LeTourneau, an Edwardsville resident and owner of the 66 Bowl, bought this original Route 66 sign from a state sale of route markers. (Courtesy of the City of Edwardsville.)

To celebrate its Mother Road heritage, Edwardsville holds an annual Route 66 festival with classic car cruises, entertainment, and the Route 66 Motor Tour. A series of articles in the *Edwardsville Intelligencer* featured images and reminiscences of local residents during one of the festivals. (Courtesy of the Edwardsville–Glen Carbon Chamber of Commerce.)

Four

MITCHELL

The Mitchell brothers—John, Jay, and William—were farmers in the present-day Mitchell area and donated land for a school and churches in the late 1800s. Apparently both a Protestant and a Catholic church were built. After years of effort to keep the Protestant church open and retain a minister, the institution came under Presbyterian management. In 1956, the old church burned, and a new one built at a different location on Chain of Rocks Road. Mitchell remains a small, unincorporated community. In recent years an attempt was made to become an independent city, but the vote failed. The Mitchell School has served children since the early 1900s; its mascot is the bulldog. Mitchell is located in the Mississippi River floodplain southwest of Edwardsville. Its main street was Route 66, along which the community's past and present businesses were and are found.

Mitchell was the location of a Route 66 split, with an early alignment headed south through Granite City, Madison, and Venice before crossing the Mississippi River and the more well-known alignment headed west from Mitchell to the Chain of Rocks Bridge. This westward route became known as Bypass 66, as, once in Missouri, motorists were able to bypass heavy city traffic in St. Louis. Mitchell boasts plenty of Route 66 history, including the Luna Café, the Bel-Air Drive-In, a row of mom-and-pop motels, and a dwindling number of neon signs. The Route 66 strip in Mitchell is oddly divided by Interstate 270; to travel the length of it, a driver must take 270 for about a mile and then exit back down to Chain of Rocks Road. At the west end of the road are the Chain of Rocks Canal Bridge, Chouteau Island wilderness area, and old Chain of Rocks river bridge.

Today the Mitchell area is visited by Route 66 enthusiasts, bicyclists or pedestrians headed for the Chain of Rocks Bridge, and locals who frequent the still-open Luna Cafe or work at the nearby Gateway Commercial Business Center.

Featuring parts and supplies for Ford Mustang automobiles, the Mustang Corral opened in 1980 at 5446 Chain of Rocks Road. Older residents remember a small triangular park with regularly mowed grass and a fireplace that once stood at this spot. (Photograph by Cheryl Eichar Jett.)

The Town and Country Motel was built around 1935 south of Edwardsville on Chain of Rocks Road. It was constructed as a pair of frame duplex cabins with front-gable roofs. The cabins and the motel sign are still visible from the road, although not in use. The sign has faded sufficiently to reveal that it had a prior life with a Kaiser-Frazer automobile dealership. (Photograph by Darren Snow.)

This postcard view of Sunset Gardens Tourist Court shows its tourist cabins in a shady spot along Route 66 about 8 miles east of the Chain of Rocks Bridge. The business had an Edwardsville telephone number. A service station also existed in connection with the tourist court. (Courtesy of Joe Sonderman.)

This trailer court is located at 732 Chain of Rocks Road. Although the fifth-wheel camper looks contemporary, the streamlined neon sign alerts Route 66 fans that this lodging was here during Route 66's heyday. (Photograph by Darren Snow.)

The Mitchell School was located on Route 66. This 1933 photograph was taken by photographer C. L. Kayser from a gas station across the road from the school; the visible-gas pump hoses can be seen at the edges of the picture. (Courtesy of Mark "Sparky" Eddleman.)

C. L. Kayser took this picture from directly in front of the Mitchell School on Route 66 on the same day he recorded the Mitchell School image. On the right side of the road is the gas station from which the photograph of Mitchell School was taken. (Courtesy of Mark "Sparky" Eddleman.)

Accidents on Route 66 became more numerous as traffic on the highway increased over the years, including on this stretch of brick-paved Route 66 through Mitchell. A 1933 photograph by an accident investigator shows a policeman standing by the right side of the road. A police car is parked on the left shoulder, and tire marks are visible on the brick pavement. The two-story building at the back right is the Luna Café. (Courtesy of Mark "Sparky" Eddleman.)

This photograph is a detail shot of the shoulder of the road shown in the previous image (about 25 feet behind the police car on the left). Apparently this disturbed section figured into the cause of the accident. The large house in the distance is now gone; a lumberyard has replaced it. (Courtesy of Mark "Sparky" Eddleman.)

The Luna Café at 201 East Chain of Rocks Road was built in 1924. According to its history, the café was frequented by gangsters such as Al Capone. People said that law-abiding citizens could not afford to eat there. There was rumored to be a gambling operation in the basement and a house of ill repute upstairs. It was said that if the cherry in the martini glass on the neon sign was lit, the girls upstairs were open for business. After more than 85 years, the Luna Café is still open for business under the same name. Today faithful local regulars and Route 66 tourists are the customers. (Above, photograph by Darren Snow; below, photograph by Cheryl Eichar Jett.)

The Mid-West Motel was located on Route 66 and Bypass U.S. 40 in Mitchell about 3 miles east of the Chain of Rocks Bridge. The "ultra-modern" motel advertised that it had electric heat and "U.S. Koylon Foam Mattresses." The construction of the Mid-West shows the transition in style from individual tourist cabins to connected motel units. (Courtesy of Joe Sonderman.)

The Bel-Air Drive-In entertained patrons from the 1950s through 1987, but was demolished in the 1990s. It opened in the mid-1950s as a single-screen drive-in, part of the St. Louis–based Mid-America Theatres chain. It was originally open year round and featured a small indoor seating area with a picture window. A second screen was added in the 1970s, and at one time, the Bel-Air could accommodate 700 cars. The sign still remains. (Photograph by Darren Snow.)

The Chain of Rocks Motel opened in 1957 at 3228 West Chain of Rocks Road with six units available for weary travelers. It is still open for business; however, the tall landmark sign was taken down a few years ago. In 1958, six units were added, with 11 more in 1960, and an additional 15 in 1977. Barbara Thoelke was the owner/operator of the lodging. (Photograph by Darren Snow.)

The Land of Lincoln is another 1950s-era Route 66 motel still sporting a big neon sign. The sign advertised phones and color TV and featured the phrase "Land of Lincoln" on a neon-outlined Illinois map. (Photograph by Darren Snow.)

The sleek and modern-looking Canal Motel and Restaurant was advertised as "nearest to the Chain of Rocks Bridge." It featured tile baths, radiant heat, air-conditioning, and television in the rooms. By the time this postcard was printed, the location was billed as "By-pass 40 and 66 (new 270)." The mailing address of this business was Granite City. (Courtesy of Joe Sonderman.)

The Twin Oaks Gas for Less station was, for a long time, travelers' last chance to gas up the family car or commercial truck before heading west across the Mississippi River. Gas for Less was a popular name for a number of independent gas stations. (Photograph by Peter Stork.)

The magnificent Chain of Rocks Bridge served the traveling public for decades before falling into disuse and consequently disrepair after the new Interstate 270 bridge was constructed just a few hundred feet away. The old bridge closed in 1968. After approximately 30 years of quiet rusting, the span has found new life as a pedestrian and bicycle path. This photograph shows the bridge from the Missouri side into Illinois. (Photograph by Peter Stork.)

Five

GRANITE CITY, MADISON, AND VENICE

Granite City was founded in 1896 as a company town by Frederick and William Niedringhaus, German immigrants who had settled in St. Louis and established the St. Louis Stamping Company, which made kitchen utensils, and the Granite Iron Rolling Mills, which provided tin. Suffering expansion challenges in St. Louis, the brothers purchased 3,500 acres across the river in the American Bottom. They enlisted a St. Louis city engineer to lay out the street grid, named the city for their enamel ware, and began Commonwealth Steel Company. To guard against the community being dependent upon one industry, other companies were encouraged to establish themselves in Granite City. Madison and Venice are two smaller communities that complete the area known as the Tri-Cities. Venice incorporated as a village in 1873 and Madison in 1891. Hard times fell on the Granite City area during the later part of the 20th century as industries closed; however, the steel mills are now back on line and running steadily.

When Route 66 was first designated in Illinois, existing roads were used. From 1926 to 1930, Route 66 ran along Gonterman Boulevard to Nameoki Road to Madison Avenue in Granite City. Along this section of Route 66 were the handsome new Granite City Community High School, beautiful new Wilson Park, steel plants, and small businesses. Madison Avenue took travelers on through Madison and Venice, where the street became Broadway, to the McKinley Bridge.

Granite City today is attempting to preserve its history in neighborhoods such as Lincoln Place. The vicinity around Wilson Park on the north side of town is notable for its well-kept historical homes. Madison is known for its joint maintenance, with Trailnet, of the Old Chain of Rocks Bridge. The span now serves as one of the world's longest bicycle and pedestrian bridges and is a vital link in the bistate trail system. It connects the Madison County Transit (MCT) Confluence Trail in Illinois with the St. Louis Riverfront Trail in Missouri. Chouteau Island, upon which the Illinois end of the Chain of Rocks Bridge rests, has been developed as a wilderness hiking trail area. Two recent attractions in Madison are the Gateway International Raceway and the Gateway National Golf Links.

These two views are of Nameoki Road along the railroad tracks near where Route 66 turned southwest onto Madison Avenue. This area of Granite City lies within Nameoki Township. The name is said to be of Native American origin and is thought to mean "smoky." A. A. Talmadge, of the Indianapolis and St. Louis Railroad, first gave the name to a railroad station in the area, and it was later adopted for the township. During the time that Route 66 passed this way, Nameoki Township was home to a number of industries, including steel, tar, fertilizer, coke, ice, and ice cream, as well as the Illinois Traction Company shops. (Photographs by C. L. Kayser; courtesy of Mark "Sparky" Eddleman.)

Wilson Park opened to the public on June 1, 1923. A special election held in February 1921 had laid the groundwork for the new Granite City Park District to be formed, and Wilson Park was its first project. Beautiful flower gardens were developed, and additional land was secured during the 1920s. In 1922, the first swimming pool was built, and the original diving tower (right) still stands. This is now known as the sunken gardens. A second pool was built in 1940 at a cost of $55,000, and the current pool opened in 1994. The park also has an ice rink. The art moderne–style park concession stand (below) is constructed of typical mid-century yellow brick. (Photographs by Darren Snow.)

This postcard view shows Granite City Community High School on Madison Avenue. The high school moved from its location on Central Avenue to this new building in 1921. Several ambitious additions over the years have accommodated the school's growth in enrollment. A 24-acre campus has allowed expansion and protected the site, which is now surrounded on two sides by commercial enterprises. (Author's collection.)

This postcard view shows St. Elizabeth Hospital in 1911. The hospital had been constructed in 1904 at a cost of $30,000, but lack of funding and management caused the institution to struggle to stay open. In the 1920s, the Sisters of Divine Providence enlarged and remodeled the hospital and established a school of nursing. About the time that Route 66 was directed elsewhere, the new St. Elizabeth Hospital was opened. (Author's collection.)

One of the first properties purchased by the park district, War Memorial Park was created when the Granite City Park District paid $6,500 for this tract across Madison Avenue from St. Elizabeth Hospital (now Gateway Medical Center). It was dedicated in 1921 as a memorial to war veterans. The fountain was added in 1961, and a major renovation was completed in 2004. (Photograph by Cheryl Eichar Jett.)

Sometime after 1900, Reinhold Seibold and his wife, Minnie, immigrated to St. Louis, where Reinhold honed his baking skills in various bakeries. In 1920, Seibold opened his own bakery in Granite City and named it Mrs. Seibold's Bake Shop. The business grew to include several locations, including Madison Avenue and Nameoki Road in Granite City and branches in East Alton, Glen Carbon, and Wood River. The last storefront location closed in 2005, but Seibold descendants still bake and sell their pastry specialties. (Photograph by Darren Snow.)

This photograph was taken at the Sinclair Service Station on Niedringhaus Avenue at Lincoln Place, close to Madison Avenue/Route 66. Part of the Commonwealth City Steel Company's complex serves as a backdrop to the image. The lettering on the building facade is "Royal Granite Steel Ware." (Courtesy of Mark "Sparky" Eddleman.)

Commonwealth Steel Co.
Granite City, Ill.

Commonwealth Steel Company was founded in 1901 and soon employed about 1,500 people, producing steel castings and railroad supplies at its 10-acre plant. The company's innovation garnered it lucrative projects such as producing steel bolsters for railroad passenger cars for the 1904 St. Louis World's Fair and manufacturing steel frames for World War I use. In 1924, a $1.5 million expansion included increasing the size of the foundry to 1,475 feet in length. (Courtesy of the Madison County Historical Society.)

The steel mills have dominated the landscape of Granite City for a century. Both of these images were taken in 1933 in the 1600 block of Madison Avenue. On this block now are Lisa's Diner and Curt's Grill. The 15-acre Commonwealth Steel Company opened in the early 1900s and by 1908 employed 2,000 men and produced 4 tons of bar steel and tinplate daily. (Both courtesy of Mark "Sparky" Eddleman.)

The McCambridge overpass carried motorists between Granite City and Madison. The image above was taken about 1941 and looks southwest toward the McCambridge overpass going from Granite City into Madison. The photograph below looks northeast from near the overpass back into Granite City. The sign on the right promotes "Hershey for governor." Harry B. Hershey was an unsuccessful Democratic candidate for governor of Illinois in 1940. He variously served as mayor of Taylorville, Illinois; Christian County state's attorney; and director of insurance of the State of Illinois. (Both courtesy of Mark "Sparky" Eddleman.)

These 1929 images show State Street from Granite City into Madison. The Madison Rotary Club's welcome sign greets motorists heading southwest along the State Street route from Granite City into Madison (above). The speed limit is posted as 15 miles per hour. The first two businesses at left are unidentified, but the third building with lettering is the Madison Planing Mill, offering millwork and building supplies. At right is part of the Commonwealth Steel Company complex. Its chimneys belch smoke into the air to the left of the railroad tracks heading northeast into Granite City (below). (Both courtesy of Mark "Sparky" Eddleman.)

Six

COLLINSVILLE

Collinsville is a historic town established in 1837 on the bluffs above the American Bottom, the floodplain of the Mississippi River, affording panoramic views across the Mississippi River to St. Louis. Collinsville's initial economy was mainly agrarian, but a coal mine begun in 1870 established a long era of mining activity. Other industries added to the town's economy through the mid-1950s. The Collinsville area produces 60 percent of the world's supply of horseradish; the Keller Farm has been growing horseradish for 100 years.

Already served by Route 40, the town added to its roster of hospitality businesses after Route 66 was realigned from Hamel to Collinsville. One alignment of Route 66 skirted Collinsville on old Route 40 via Vandalia Street. It then went west on what is now known as Belt Line Road for about 2 miles before turning south again on what is now State Route 157/Bluff Road along the bluffs upon which most of Collinsville is built. At Collinsville Road, Route 66 again moved west down onto the floodplain. In the 1960s, Interstate 55 was constructed north and west of Collinsville.

Along this route was a large and well-appointed restaurant, the Evergreen Gardens, which eventually became a church, and a Standard Oil service station with an art deco tower atop it. Fairmount Park, Cahokia Mounds State Park, and the Falcon Drive-In Theatre lie farther out from town along Route 66/Route 40. A few early cabins and motels dotted this alignment. Eventually national chain motels arrived. The Best Western Round Table Motor Lodge, Howard Johnson's Motor Lodge, and Holiday Inn all presaged the day when a lineup of national chain motels and restaurants would jockey for the best positions near the Interstate 55/70 exit.

Collinsville is known today for Cahokia Mounds State Historic Site and the Brooks Catsup Bottle water tower and as the crossroads of major Metro East highways. The self-proclaimed "Horseradish Capital of the World," Collinsville is also the home of Fairmount Park. Old Route 40 is marked with a series of signs that indicate its National Road history.

John's Mobil Service Center was located at 2000 Vandalia Street in the 1970s. John Finley was the proprietor and offered automobile services including towing, brakes, mufflers, shocks, and complete SUN tune-ups. Postcards like this one reminded customers that it had been 60 days since their last oil change. The next proprietor was Al Tognarelli, who changed the name to Al's Mobil Service. (Courtesy of Collinsville History Museum.)

Fritz and Liz Luksan operated Zeppetella's Italian Restaurant at 1813 Vandalia Street in Collinsville for over 30 years on the block just before Route 66 turned west on Route 40, now known as Belt Line Road. The restaurant advertised chicken, steaks, and Italian food as their specialties. (Courtesy of Collinsville History Museum.)

This postcard dated 1956 shows the Pines Lounge and Motel on Cuba Lane as it looked when it opened about 1948. The street address is now 416 Belt Line Road. The location became the home of the Red Bar in 2009. (Courtesy of the Collinsville History Museum.)

Howard Johnson's Motor Lodge was located adjacent to the new Interstate 55/70, Route 66, and State Route 157. The motor lodge promised "91 luxurious rooms, cocktail lounge, restaurant, air conditioned, heated pool, TV, meeting and banquet rooms." (Courtesy of the Collinsville History Museum.)

The Brooks Catsup Bottle water tower was built in 1949 for the G. S. Suppiger bottling plant, bottlers of Brooks Catsup. The 170-foot tower holds 100,000 gallons of water. The Catsup Bottle Preservation Group saved the structure from demolition and restored it to its original appearance in 1995. In 2002, it was added to the National Register of Historic Places. Although not on the Collinsville Route 66 alignment, it was surely seen by tourists of that era, as it is now. (Photograph by Michael Gassmann; courtesy of World's Largest Catsup Bottle, Inc.)

The Round Table Lodge and Restaurant (above) offered travelers 82 rooms, a restaurant, and a long list of amenities at its location near Interstate 55/70 at the corner of Mall and Bluff Roads (Route 157). Some of the attractions the complex offered included cinema, meeting rooms, an animal shelter, babysitters, a playground, valet service, car rental, laundry on premises, a sauna and steam bath, camper facilities, color television, a swimming pool, queen-size beds, and private in-room bars. After 12 years in business, the restaurant in the photograph at right of the multi-view card was destroyed by fire in 1981. Later the motel was used as the Round Table Professional Center and has since been turned into an apartment building. (Both courtesy of the Collinsville History Museum.)

Also adjacent to the new Interstate 55/70 and State Route 157 was the Holiday Inn of Collinsville. This motel featured an "indoor recreation center for all-weather fun," with a pool, hot tub, shuffleboard, putting green, and relaxation areas, all under a large roof protecting travelers from inclement weather. (Courtesy of the Collinsville History Museum.)

EVERGREEN GARDENS
For Reservations, Phone 1500

On U. S. Highways 40, Belt Line
40 and 157, Collinsville, Ill.

Old churches are sometimes converted into restaurants, but in the case of Evergreen Gardens, the reverse was true. This very large and very popular restaurant offered five spacious dining rooms to accommodate wedding receptions and banquets. The Evergreen Gardens is seen here as it appeared in 1945. In the 1960s, the Church of the Nazarene made the beautiful building its home and still occupies it. (Courtesy of the Collinsville History Museum.)

Just past Evergreen Gardens at the intersection of Collinsville and Bluff Roads was this Standard Oil service station with an art deco tower. The back of this postcard advertised the "best transient service in the Middlewest." On this site now is Ramon's Restaurant. (Courtesy of the Collinsville History Museum.)

The Rainbo Court Motel was located at 5280 Collinsville Road, "five miles from downtown St. Louis on Hwy. 40." The motel offered 30 modern units with tile baths, carpet, electric heat, air-conditioning, television, and phones. (Courtesy of the Collinsville History Museum.)

The Fairmount Jockey Club opened on September 26, 1925, on what had previously been Edwards' hog farm. About 9,000 people braved pouring rain to attend the first day of racing. A horse named Seth's Alibi won the feature race and paid $4.70 for a $2 "subscription." Betting was illegal at that time, but subscriptions could be made toward the winner's purse, with some financial returns going to the contributors. (Courtesy of the Collinsville History Museum.)

Fairmount Race Track was not the only racing facility in the Collinsville area. Another racecourse had been built around 1900 on the Kneedler farm; it evolved into League Park, used by high school sports teams and local baseball teams. A. Sumner also built an early track at the north end of Sumner Boulevard. The Cahokia Downs Racetrack opened in 1954. (Courtesy of the Collinsville History Museum.)

In 1950, for the first time in the country's history, Fairmount offered racing under the lights, which cost $100,000 to install. At its peak, the track employed 500 people, including jockeys, trainers, owners, stable workers, concessionaires, and ticket sellers. In 1969, Ogden Corporation of New York purchased Fairmount as part of a multimillion dollar deal that included other racetracks and sport facilities. (Courtesy of the Collinsville History Museum.)

Fairmount Race Track suffered a number of tornados and fires over the years. In both 1952 and 1953, tornados removed the grandstand roof. A barn fire in August 1972 took the lives of 18 thoroughbred horses. Another fire broke out in April 1974 on the day before a contract dispute was to be settled. Over 1,000 horses were saved, but the grandstand and equipment suffered an estimated $6 million in damages. (Courtesy of the Collinsville History Museum.)

The images on these two pages are from a postal folder advertising the Mounds Country Club and Garden in the late 1940s. Schmidt's Mound Park had been the predecessor to this establishment and was built in the late 1800s a quarter mile east of Monks Mound. Schmidt's two-story inn became the center section of the Mounds Country Club, which opened after renovations and additions in the 1920s. (Courtesy of the Collinsville History Museum.)

This view shows the Mounds Club Garden Terrace. The original known owners were East St. Louis bookmaker Frank Waller, bootlegger Harry Murdock, and East Side gangster William "Bow-wow" McQuillan, although Frank "Buster" Wortman, bootlegger and Shelton Brothers Gang member, was rumored to also be a partner. The advertising folder promoted the Mounds Club's "nationally known $1.00 chicken dinner." (Courtesy of the Collinsville History Museum.)

TWO DE LUXE SHOWS NIGHTLY WITH ALL STAR CAST SA-H1494

"Two de luxe shows nightly with all star cast" is the caption on this image. Stars like Rudy Vallee and Sophie Tucker performed at the Mounds Club. Gambling was also a big attraction. An article by Virginia Irwin in the *St. Louis Post-Dispatch* stated, "It was considered the most elaborate and wide-open gambling house south of Chicago. It was patronized by society figures, businessmen, members of the racetrack fraternity, prosperous bootleggers, and the cream of the East Side underworld." (Courtesy of the Collinsville History Museum.)

LARGEST OUTDOOR DANCE FLOOR IN MIDDLE WEST SA-H1491

The club boasted that it could accommodate 2,500 people and that it had the "largest outdoor dance floor in Middle West," as seen on this postcard. Jack Langer managed the Mounds Club at the time this folder was produced. It closed in the 1950s and became an office for Grandpa's Discount Store. A few years later, the once-elegant club was razed, replaced by a parking lot. (Courtesy of the Collinsville History Museum.)

In 1925, the State of Illinois purchased 144 acres of the Ramey family land to establish Cahokia Mounds State Park. This Southwestern-style building was constructed to serve as the ranger's residence, with one room devoted to exhibits. In the early 1970s, an agreement between the Illinois State Museum and the Department of Conservation allowed a new staff, led by curator Jim Anderson and assistant William Iseminger, to develop interpretive and educational programs. The building was gutted, and interpretive spaces were created. Soon the staff had created over 30 exhibits, a small theater, and a gift shop. They also built house reconstructions and experimental gardens. After the construction of a new world-class interpretive center in 1989, the old museum was razed. (Courtesy of Cahokia Mounds State Historic Site.)

This view of Monks Mound taken around 1940 shows the 14-acre mound covered with trees; they have since been removed. Locals in the area began calling it Monks Mound after a group of Trappist monks settled in the area. The rectangular-shaped mound is, at approximately 100 feet tall, the largest man-made earthen mound in the Americas. Route 40 (Collinsville Road)— also used for a period of time as Route 66—can be seen at the lower right. (Courtesy of Cahokia Mounds State Historic Site.)

This aerial view looking west along Route 40/66 taken about 1922 shows Monks Mound just to the right of the road. The Twin Mounds are clearly visible in the large field at left, opposite Monks Mound. Archaeologists now know that the large area between the Twin Mounds and Monks Mound served as a plaza for gatherings, games, and activities for the Mississippian culture that once lived here. (Courtesy of Cahokia Mounds State Historic Site.)

Looking east from Cahokia Mounds back toward Collinsville, Monks Mound is at left in the bottom of the photograph, and the Twin Mounds are near the right. Founded as Cahokia Mounds State Park in 1925, it was reclassified as Cahokia Mounds State Historic Site about 1980. In 1982, the site was designated a United Nations Educational, Scientific, and Cultural Organization (UNESCO) World Heritage Site. A world-class, $8.2 million interpretive center was built and opened in 1989. (Courtesy of Cahokia Mounds State Historic Site.)

E. G. Vogt Sales and Service was located at 6001 Collinsville Road on Route 40 just past Cahokia Mounds State Park. At the time of this photograph, this large service station featured five islands of pumps and three service bays. Vogt advertised "complete one-stop Skelly service, U.S. Royal and Hood tires, car washing and greasing, automotive supplies, electrical appliances, Admiral radio and television, refrigerators and electric ranges." (Courtesy of the Collinsville Historical Museum.)

The Falcon Drive-In Theater was located at 7400 Collinsville Road; the site was part of the ancient Mississippian culture's civilization now called Cahokia Mounds and is now included in the historic site's tract of land. The Falcon was torn down after the State of Illinois acquired the land to add to Cahokia Mounds State Historic Site. (Courtesy of Cahokia Mounds State Historic Site.)

G. E. M. (Government Employees Mart) Department Store opened at this location in the 1960s; G. E. M. was a chain of discount stores that extended membership to government employees. The company was defunct by 1973. Next to inhabit the building was the Venture department and discount store, one of about 70 in the chain. The building became home to Gateway Classic Cars in 1999. (Photograph by Cheryl Eichar Jett.)

Seven

THE BRIDGES

The McKinley Bridge opened in 1910, named for its builder William B. McKinley, chief executive of the Illinois Traction System electric railway. For many years the bridge carried both vehicular and railroad traffic across the Mississippi River. The McKinley Bridge served the first alignment of Route 66 from 1926 to 1930. The route to the bridge followed State Route 203 through Granite City, Madison, and Venice.

The Municipal Bridge, popularly known as the "Free Bridge," was constructed in 1917 by the City of St. Louis to break a monopoly of the railroad association that controlled the other two bridges. This bridge was used as the second alignment of Route 66 across the Mississippi River from 1929 until the mid-1930s. In the early 1940s, it was renamed the Gen. Douglas MacArthur Bridge.

The Chain of Rocks Bridge was constructed in 1929 to carry Route 66 traffic around the heart of St. Louis. Its unique 22-degree bend at the middle is remembered by many baby boomers as being the cause for getting stuck on the bridge for hours at a time. Accidents and large trucks or trailers often caused traffic jams. Route 66 went directly west from the town of Mitchell to cross the river, offering travelers Bypass 66 to avoid St. Louis city traffic.

The Veterans Memorial Bridge, later renamed the Martin Luther King Bridge, was built in 1951 to relieve the congestion on the MacArthur Bridge. It then carried the fourth alignment of Route 66 from Collinsville through Fairmont City and East St. Louis to this Mississippi River crossing. After the Poplar Street Bridge opened in 1967, the Martin Luther King Bridge lost much of its traffic and toll revenue, causing it to fall into disrepair.

The last of the five bridges to carry Route 66 out of Illinois was the Bernard F. Dickmann/Poplar Street Bridge. Named for St. Louis mayor Dickmann, the bridge became known by the street over which the end of the bridge sits. This bridge officially carried Route 66 from 1967 to 1977. As travelers crossed the Mississippi River into another leg of their journey, they surely did not soon forget the people they met or the places they stopped in Madison County.

The McKinley Bridge is a steel-truss bridge and is 6,313 feet long. Originally built for railroad use, wings were added in 1926 to accommodate vehicular traffic, which was charged a toll. The bridge was out of service from 2001 until 2007. It was first reopened for bicyclists and pedestrians, but vehicular traffic access was once again added. (Author's collection.)

The Municipal Bridge was built in 1917 and soon became known as the "Free Bridge." It is a three-span through-truss bridge that is 2,022 feet in length. In the early 1940s, it was designated the Gen. Douglas MacArthur Bridge, which remains its official name. This bridge was built by the City of St. Louis at a cost of $6 million. (Author's collection.)

The Chain of Rocks Bridge is a cantilever through-truss bridge with a total length of 5,353 feet and a width of 24 feet. The cost to build the toll bridge was $3 million in the late 1920s. It was named for the rocky rapids in that part of the river, which were known to be dangerous to navigate. The need to allow uninterrupted river traffic and the availability of land on the Missouri shore were issues that ultimately resulted in the 22-degree bend in the bridge. The Chain of Rocks was the third bridge alignment for Route 66 across the Mississippi River. The span now carries biking and walking trails and was placed on the National Register of Historic Places in 2006. (Courtesy of the Madison County Historical Society.)

The Veterans' Memorial Bridge was constructed in 1951 and refurbished in 1987 after a lengthy period of disrepair. This is a cantilever truss bridge and is 4,009 feet long and 40 feet wide. This bridge was originally owned by the city of East St. Louis, but joint control was eventually transferred to the Illinois and Missouri Departments of Transportation. Although this was a toll bridge for many years, the toll was removed in 1987. It was later renamed the Martin Luther King Bridge. (Author's collection.)

The Bernard F. Dickmann Bridge opened in 1967 and was named for a former St. Louis mayor, but the common name is the Poplar Street Bridge. It is a steel-girder bridge and is 2,164 feet in length and 104 feet in width to accommodate multiple lanes of traffic. Route 66 motorists used this bridge from 1967 until 1977, when Interstate 55 and other numbered highways took over the bridge. (Photograph by Erica Jett.)

BIBLIOGRAPHY

"60 Years of Exceptional Service: Klueter Brothers Concrete Products, Edwardsville, Illinois." Besser Concrete Impressions. Alpena, MI: Besser Company. 6.1 (First Quarter 2007).

Alexander, Brian L. "Which Bridge Did I Cross?" Route 66 Association of Illinois: The 66 News, Spring 2010.

Brown, Sharon A. *Jefferson National Expansion Administrative History*. National Park Service, 1984.

Canepa, Hella. "Chain of Rocks Bridge." *Route 66 Magazine* 4 no.1 (Winter 1996/97).

Cassens, Albert. *The History of Cassens Transport*. Edwardsville, IL: Cassens, 1996.

Collinsville Historical Museum. *Collinsville*. Edited by Neal Strebel. Charleston, SC: Arcadia Publishing, 2005.

Edwardsville Historic Preservation Commission oral histories.

Granite City, A Pictorial History, 1896–1996. Granite City, IL: G. Bradley Publishing, 1995.

Illinois Route 66 Scenic Byway Visitors Guide 2009. Springfield, IL: Illinois Route 66 Scenic Byway, 2009.

Iseminger, William R. *Cahokia Mounds: America's First City*. Charleston, SC: History Press, 2010.

Jett, Cheryl Eichar. *Postcard History Series: Edwardsville*. Chicago, IL: Arcadia Publishing, 2009.

Livingston, Illinois, Centennial Committee. *Livingston, Illinois History*. Livingston, IL: Livingston, Illinois, Centennial Committee, 2005.

Nore, Ellen, and Dick Norrish. *Edwardsville: An Illustrated History*. St. Louis, MO: G. Bradley Publishing, 1996.

Rittenhouse, Jack DeVere. *A Guide Book to Highway 66*. Albuquerque, NM: University of New Mexico Press, 1989. First published 1946 by Jack Rittenhouse.

Weiss, John. *Traveling the . . . New, Historic Route 66 of Illinois*. Wilmington, IL: John Weiss, 1997.

http://bridgehunter.com (Historic Bridges of the United States)

www.arcadiapublishing.com

MAP SEARCH

Discover books about the town where you grew up, the cities where your friends and families live, the town where your parents met, or even that retirement spot you've been dreaming about. Our Web site provides history lovers with exclusive deals, advanced notification about new titles, e-mail alerts of author events, and much more.

Find Your Place in History.